Really Wild
WHALES

Claire Robinson

Heinemann
LIBRARY

First published in Great Britain by Heinemann Library,
Halley Court, Jordan Hill, Oxford OX2 8EJ,
a division of Reed Educational and Professional Publishing Ltd.

Heinemann is a registered trademark of Reed Educational & Professional Publishing Limited.

OXFORD MELBOURNE AUCKLAND
JOHANNESBURG BLANTYRE GABORONE
IBADAN PORTSMOUTH NH (USA) CHICAGO

Designed by Celia Floyd
Illustrations by Alan Fraser (Pennant Illustration)
Colour reproduction by Dot Gradations
Printed and bound in Hong Kong/China

04 03 02 01 00
10 9 8 7 6 5 4 3 2 1

ISBN 0 431 02887 7

British Library Cataloguing in Publication Data

Robinson, Claire
Whale. – (Really wild) (Take-off!)
1. Whales – Juvenile literature
I. Title
599.5

Look at the whale at the bottom of each page. Flick the pages and see what happens!

Acknowledgements
The Publishers would like to thank the following for permission to reproduce photographs:
Ardea London Ltd: Francois Gohier, pp.4 (left and right), p.9, 11, 12-13, 18, 20, 22, Mike Osmond p.7, Jean-Paul Ferrero p.14, J.M La Roque p.17; Bruce Coleman: Mr Johnny Johnson p.15; Natural History Unit: Doc White pp.8, 16, 19, 23; Oxford Scientific Films: Zig Leszczynski p.5 (left), Mark Newman p.5 (right), Ben Osborne p.6, C.J. Gilbert p.10, Duncan Murrell p.21.

Cover photograph: Tony Stone Images/Stuart Westmorland

Our thanks to Sue Graves for her advice and expertise in the preparation of this book.

Every effort has been made to contact copyright holders of any material reproduced in this book. Any omissions will be rectified in subsequent printings if notice is given to the Publisher.

For more information about Heinemann Library books, or to order, please telephone +44(0)1865 888066, or send a fax to +44(0)1865 314091. You can visit our website at www.heinemann.co.uk

Contents

Some words are shown in bold, **like this**. You can find out what they mean by looking in the glossary.

Whale relatives

Whales are large **mammals** that live in the sea. They are warm-blooded animals. They have to keep warm all the time. Whales have a layer of fat, called **blubber**, to keep them warm in cold waters.

Grey whales have baleen instead of teeth.

A male sperm whale can grow up to 20 metres long.

A beluga whale is also called a white whale.

Humpback whales like to leap out of the water like this.

There are many kinds of whale, but only two main groups. One group has teeth and the other group has **baleen**. Humpback whales are one of the larger baleen whales. Let's see how they live.

Where do whales live?

Humpback whales can be found in all of the oceans around the world. They spend most of the year in the icy cold seas around the **Arctic** and **Antarctic**. There is plenty of food for whales to eat in these seas.

whales

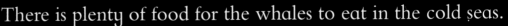
There is plenty of food for the whales to eat in the cold seas.

These whales are swimming to warmer waters before winter arrives.

Whales **migrate** to warmer waters when it is time to **mate** and give birth. Whales in the Arctic swim south. Whales in the Antarctic swim north.

7

Diving and breathing

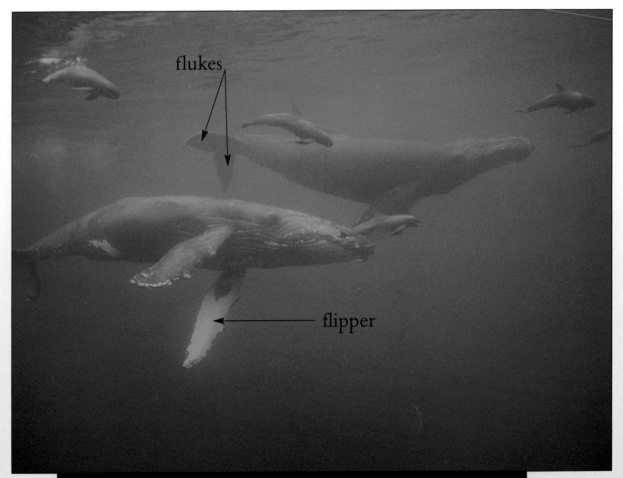

flukes

flipper

Whales use their powerful tails to help them to swim.

Whales swim by moving their tails up and down. Long flippers help them turn and dive. They can stay underwater for half an hour between breaths.

The tail fin is split into two paddle shapes called flukes.

spout

blowhole

This whale is breathing out through its blowhole.

Whales cannot breathe under the sea. They have to come to the surface to breathe air. When whales breathe out through their **blowholes**, water on top of their head is blown upwards in a spout.

Finding food

The cold seas are full of good food. Whales like to eat lots of tiny animals called **krill**. Krill look like small shrimps.

The most common type of krill looks like this.

There are 600 trillion of the most common type of krill.

The whale shoots upwards in the water with its mouth wide open. Its throat stretches wider as it fills up with krill.

This whale trap as much krill as it can in its wide open mouth.

Eating

whale baleen

mouth

These whales have baleen inside their mouths to trap krill.

These whales do not have teeth. They have **baleen** inside their mouths instead. Baleen is whalebone. It is like a big sieve that traps the **krill** inside, but lets the water out.

bubble net

whales with mouths
wide open

These whales are feeding together. They trap
the krill by blowing a bubble net. The whales
swim inside the ring of bubbles to eat the krill.

Migrating

This school of whales is swimming to warmer seas for the winter.

As winter draws near, the humpback whales **migrate** in groups to warmer seas hundreds of miles away. They go there to **mate**.

A group of whales is called a school.

eye

Humpback whales can sometimes be seen near the coast.

Humpback whales like to swim near the **coast**. Sometimes, they poke their heads out of the water to look around. Look how small the whale's eye is.

Baby whales

When a male wants to **mate**, he sings strange songs. He hopes the females will hear and come to mate. It will be 11 months before a baby whale is born.

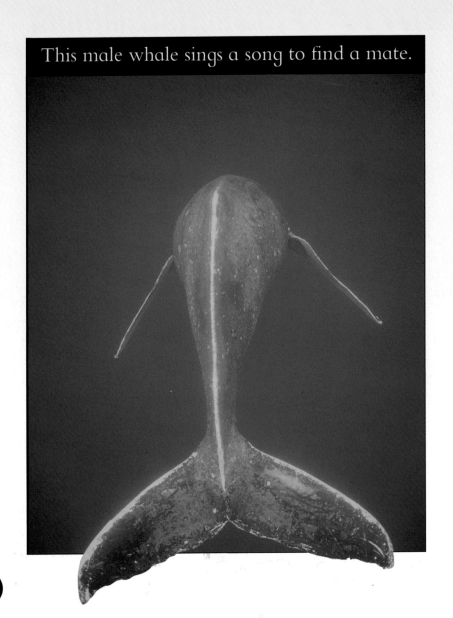
This male whale sings a song to find a mate.

A humpback whale only has one baby whale at a time. A baby whale is called a **calf**. This calf is one week old. As soon as he was born, his mother pushed him to the surface so that he could breathe in air.

This calf is only one week old.

Growing up

This mother whale and her calf are migrating to colder waters.

The whale **calf** stays close to his mother. In spring, they **migrate** back to the cold seas with the other humpback whales.

This whale is breaching.

As they grow up, whales learn how to find **krill**, and how to hold their breath as they dive. They also like to leap right out of the water. This is called breaching.

Whales and people

Whales, like these, were hunted for their oil.

Humpback whales are gentle giants. In the past, people have hunted these whales for the oil in their **blubber** and for their meat. Thousands of whales were killed every year. Now there are not many left.

Whales can be very big. This whale's tail is as wide as a car! A humpback whale can weigh about 66 tons.

This whale's tail is as wide as a car.

Humpback whale facts

- Whales are **mammals**; they feed their babies on milk and breathe air like humans.

- Humpback whales have no teeth. Instead, they sieve their food through 350 layers of **baleen**.

- Humpback whales can live for up to 95 years.

You can spot a humpback whale because of its humped back and the lumps on its head.

They have very long flippers that are white underneath and have lumpy edges.

flipper

- A humpback whale can weigh 66 tons.

- Humpback whales sing very complicated songs. Their songs can last up to 5 minutes each. The sound they make can be heard many kilometres away, through the water.

- Humpback whales can grow up to 16 metres (46 feet) long.

Glossary

Arctic   the cold, northern tip of the world

Antarctic   the cold, southern tip of the world

baleen   a fringe of stiff layers that acts as a sieve

blowhole   nostrils on top of a whale's head

blubber   fat on a whale's body

calf   a baby whale

coast   land near the sea

krill   tiny sea animals that look like shrimps

mammal   a warm-blooded animal that feeds its babies on milk, some mammals have hair

mate   to find or be a partner to have babies with

migrate   make a long journey every year

Index